These lyrics dare to "b
and blues of race snafu
intellectual analysis, ha
insights. They come fr
gradations connecting black skin to white, pop culture to academia, and link sophisticated analysis with the verve and drive of performance poetry.

~ Dektet Jury

ex nihilo

ADEBE D.A.

To Paulo,
With all my heart and with thanks for gracing this book (and my life) with your support + presence.

Frontenac House
Calgary, Alberta

Book and cover design: Epix Design
Cover image: Photograph by David Reyes
Author photo: Ogilvy and Mather, New York

Library and Archives Canada Cataloguing in Publication

D.A., Adebe
Ex nihilo / Adebe D.A.

Poems.
ISBN 978-1-897181-34-8

I. Title.

PS8607.A13E95 2010 C811'.6 C2009-907341-2

We acknowledge the support of the Canada Council for the Arts for our publishing program and the support of the Alberta Creative Development Initiative. We also acknowledge the support of The Alberta Foundation for the Arts.

Canada Council for the Arts Conseil des Arts du Canada

Alberta Foundation for the Arts

Printed and bound in Canada
Published by Frontenac House Ltd.
1138 Frontenac Avenue S.W.
Calgary, Alberta, T2T 1B6, Canada
Tel: 403-245-2491 Fax: 403-245-2380
editor@frontenachouse.com www.frontenachouse.com

To the inventors of souls
who have always believed
in creation ex nihilo
as a response.

Acknowledgements

To the jury of Dektet, and my fellow literary comrades across generations and borders who know who they are – your support is everything.

To Amiri Baraka, for teaching me how to fight and write against "spontaneous ignorance," and your mentorship.

To Anne Waldman, for your incredible vision and vitality during my time at the Jack Kerouac School, Naropa University.

To my Professors for their insight and outstanding support of my academic and creative work – in particular, Vermonja R. Alston, Marcia Blumberg, B.W. Powe, Art Redding, Leslie Sanders, and Priscila Uppal.

To the Ontario Arts Council for their generous support through the Writers' Reserve Grant.

And foremost to my family, and Alex DeRango, with love.

Contents

Ex Nihilo

English Literature

Why,
Because *chiaroscuro*
is where I belong.
That and I was once Pushkin's wife.
O, my darling octoroon
your Russia is doing alive and well,
but your Ethiopia is still squinting into the sun,
blind and full of light
trying to find empire in uptown Harlem
but all we get is
gentrification petrification talk
about holy war, race war, war on war
while the Church of Nazareth on 144th stands
a burned-out shell, waiting.

Concealed Things

colour in the mechanism
of concealment,
lineage a dangerous dream

of children marked forever
into the gaze,
pushed into alleyways

roads, orchards, skylines;
but look closely,
in these whole anthropological worlds

you may find my people –
they look like yours,
merged in the pure gaze of the sun

with Exodus in their eyes,
being taught to believe
there is no other world.

Colour Lessons

I.

Family Studies, age ten:

when asked what colour
I thought described who I was
I wrote down "everything"

a chameleon, cool and smooth
but the class laughed
and my teacher asked
why would I want to be that

so that I can *be* anything,
I replied

years later
my blond highlights
do all the talking, and are
definitely more fun

less work and less laughter,
the rest of the animal kingdom
now quiet and aroused
by my silence,
and less chaos

II.

The academic in me is waiting
for the time when contours dissolve
and bodies really don't matter.

The artist in me
when flesh becomes abstraction
becomes song,

not something that falls
between the cracks
or stalls, tries to pass

but when flesh becomes dance
a body that can turn to itself and say
    What will it be? *What will we be*

and then everything
crumbling
into legitimate freedom.

Open Letter

dear half-bloods,
half-castes
half-breeds,
cross-breeds
miscegenates,
alvinos
cabres,
castizos
cholos,
chinos
creoles,
dustees
fustees,
griffes
mamalucos,
marabouts
mestees,
mestizos
misterados,
mongrels
moriscos,
mustafinas
mustees,
ochavons
octavons,
octoroons
puchuelos,
quadroons

quarterons,
quatralvis
quinterons,
saltatros
tercerons,
zambaigos
zambos,
and for all the others who passed –
tell me
who failed you?

Ex Libris

I come from the land of
Where You From?
My people dispossessed of their stories
and who have died again and again
in a minstrelsy of afterlives, wakes,
the dead who walk, waiting and
furrowed, like ivy crawling up

All those museums and mausoleums,
lifting languages from rivers.
But I cannot leave them
for the rugged North
nor the hot-blooded South south of us,
nor the untamed deltas
that plaster us to our jackets

My road is neither smooth nor gravel,
my destination neither cathedral nor whole.
I am learning
all about ex-colonial States and states,
the oblivion of my fate
and the legacy of the Veil
from sea to shining sea, drowning
in the calm of our Great Lakes

And the orphan angels
who crowd our classrooms:
I see them, heartless & disrespected
each page burning as it gets read,
and their othered faces burning to tell the others
this ain't nobody's Atlantic!
we don't have to keep on dyin' in books!

An English Degree

might not get me more than a ticket to a poetry reading,
illuminate what is great white and blinding, and obsessed

with death. Worded differently, it might be a free ride
to the center of some galaxy where the entire history

of literature becomes the poem we are reading, the
microcosm of every word a journey from hieroglyph

to the first manifestation of thought. With difficulty I grasp what
I was taught to have been the necessity of letting go,

of seeing the total order of words, the vision that cannot be sold
with magazine subscriptions or to editors

in some corner of New Brunswick. It might very well be the wick
made waterproof, made to fire forever

in the minds of each generation, the other necessity being to
throw myth to flame. It may not get me fame or a fancy

tomb in Paris, but then again I am not looking to sleep. Perhaps
it is just metaphorical, standing for the object

afraid to look itself in the face, in all those permutations of
beauty and faith. A way of making sense of the oppressive

space between us, between objects and you and I, something that
speaks to us both in a whisper

before the storm and yells from the frame of this degree,
hanging like art. Thankfully something to hold on to and

unto: the last key to this dysmorphic universe,
the last metaphor to affirm another world

is always possible.

New World

the cosmos continually pushing
me to refuse doubleness,
to slap la patria across the face

the inheritors who don't believe in real colour
only the exotic ones
that accompany festivals and parades

somewhere

Isis cries,
tears melding with Nile

a place where I was not born
but have been to before,
that place where Marquez still tangos
and Dante forever renews himself

my thousand-year-old self
still waiting

to refuse the Veil
and drink the blackberry wines
of the known and unknown women

of my birth,
women who perhaps were
empresses

singing opaque songs
of love and knowing
exactly how their men loved

harlots,
absolving them
in incantations of frankincense,

coffee beans, finding
happiness from the edges,
from the night's masquerades of love

their thankfully stillborn
children of Ham
the only survivors

young girls and boys singing
from the edges
watching us blissed out below,
lost.

I Am Not Cleopatra

You want history, to tuck me into bed
with lessons of Sekhemkhet, Narmer,

to forget this moment when we are touching,
like history always does in the manner

of amnesia. You call upon old lovers
for conversation as I listen with patience,

attest to their womanly ghosts with a
wringing out of wrists: their imagined

measurements, the facts of their limbs.
I await your testament and you wait for me

to blink from behind a papyrus with
eyes of Nefertiti, a blue glaze across the terra

cotta of my skin like a soft, tragic laugh, as if
my only desire is to become part of the ancient

paraphernalia, die with a heart intemperate
as a dune. You will remember the black sky

of my hair by morning when it is washed out
with the pale sun; you will remember my skin's

dynasty when it falls from your hands. But I am
not truly Cleopatra and your visions of me are

as soft as the prosopopoeia of my mouth burning
in silent sharp shapes. I have never cared for amulets

or to draw tricks from my sleeves, and have little heart
to hear you speak of religion and methods, long not to be

Cleopatra, waiting for the moment to disarm or conquer
you in a bravado of smoke, which is too easy. So let us

forget searching, even if digging is the only method for depth, for
the necessary drowning, each night

the wild reverberation of names. Many a night I heard you speak
my name in a ringing out of time, and then turn back

in a gesture of madness or frailty, and so dethrone me
from your love. But here I am speaking about the future,

turning myself into ghost which is perhaps how
you wanted it: to apprehend my figure, the pitch of its sigh

in a song of sarcophagi, to pretend my eyes
bear the sadness of rivers, from Dire-Dawa to Damascus,

melt as we do into sand. When I turn to you
you are still looking for Cleopatra, want me dead

or at least without questions, to answer you
in tongues, mouths, negotiate in dark choreographies,

old utterances echoing back. If you want history
the best I can do is let you go

in the style of Exodus, which reads
one should not permit a sorceress to live.

Instead I will acquire another method
of alchemy, learn to turn your body

to brimstone without touching, to withhold
questions, speak in incantations only,

create an empire from dust.

Anonymous Wuz a Womahn

1956 – anonymous wuz a womahn
who marched to Pretoria wid a queshun
and burned her pass law papers,
documents to prove she wuz human

anonymous wuz a womahn
treated like subhuman,
even now dere iz still so much confusion
dat make freedom feel an illusion

but if ya strike da womahn ya strike da rock
anonymous iz still a womahn
learning how to walk and talk and write in 1956
hailing from the time ma mother wuz born

dere wuz womahnz an ocean ova
marching wid war torn babes on they backs
fighting pass laws,
and anonymous iz still womahn fighting da need to pass

to be thrown into a class below grass
a class o' good-as-dead
who will never git ahead
anonymous iz womahn who invades ma bloody head

who comes to me from da shore drained o' self
unable to speak for her werdz iz somewhere else;
anonymous iz black womahn white woman mixed-up womahn

whose body wuz never in da minds
o' the generations destroyed by madness
as ya heard in 1956, and whose hip limbs wuz never dragged
through da so-called negro streets at dawn

looking for an empty fix, nah time for tricks;
anonymous has been every black womahn
whose black looks inspired hooks
to analyze oppression as it affects both you and I

and for all those for whom the bell tolls,
for anonymous iz all our mothers who walked away
unknown and forgotten into da ghostly daze,
anonymous iz da womahn o' everyday

cries ya will hear in da blaze:
she may come drenched in history
but she iz still one for fire,
fires dat do not speak o' love

fires dat would sober up Bukowski
fires dat march in rhythms o' blood;
anonymous iz a womahn wit unforgiving blood,
who iz gold and wax, all origins

o' humanity, dis here story iz one ya gots heard before
but her story iz one ya can't hear
less ya learn ghost talk,
the proper way to carry dem bones,

bones o' broken-up rhyme, stones o' dat earth
dat ya walk over each time,
anonymous iz a womahn who dies
so ya may be alive;

iz everything dat wuz ever written, every poet
who has been born,
iz da missing link o' freedom for those

who made it cross da shore;
anonymous iz a womahn who cannot be made into poem
anonymous iz a womahn who iz so much more

than time will allow to repair
and history can let us rewrite;
anonymous iz a womahn who embodies
dis here fight

every document signed anonymous
wuz a womahn,
wuz nahh one, wuz each o' us; ya cannot dig womahn
cuz she iz not waiting for you to dig, ya dig

ya cannot contain womahn,
she will not let you colonize her land,
da body o' dis here poem iz not even her body,
for what body can I speak of?

dere iz only image
holy ghost of masculine trinity
all else anonymity

anonymous womahn without body
or speech, and also every body
o' speech dat screams,
every bloody mary

iz every textuality burned up,
iz every unknown entity
and when I peep in da mirror what do I see

I can feel da lines in ma hands
like border zones, frontlines
can read all her missing headlines

I can hear da sea
pouring out into da river
like praisesong

dere iz something walking across da water
like a womahn

and finally I see
my reflection, see her in me

she iz giving me dis here chance
to burn free.

Listening to Coltrane in NY, Post-9/11

It's a mystery – man's direst aspirations
clothing themselves in reason, women and their green
fields bursting lonely flowers with a veil for skin,
torment for bliss HERE YES HERE but dear earth
I'm not there – that was you thirty years
ago and now fragile lines forming at the center of
our speech stitching memories in, trying not to forget
that myths don't kill people, people do, and how
do I let go now by the flow of some syncopated tune,
what river is there to speak to, how can I sing
and what language is there for silence

Haiku for Baraka

The pitch is this:
socialism is just like feminism
except that it's actually
helping people

I wonder:
were my past lives
as good poems
as your past wives?

Beethoven must have passed
for deaf, too, and Du Bois
only pretended
to accept

They said you left early
cuz your family was getting arrested
in Jersey,
and that you sighed

When yr finished yr book, drop it off
you said,
and now suddenly so many
books to write

Ragtime Bourgeoisie

yep that's me
be-bop in university
classrooms
using n-apostrophes and essentially
existentially free

though my parents were
refugees
they also came uncolonized,
arrived with Romanesque noses
making sure

I would never be naked
crazy or starving,
so I grew up drinkin' coffee
with Buddha on my mind

I am still with mind/body
cuz neither was destroyed
ran away
or was forced to
buy itself back/
I am voluntarily Black

you like my jive? my joy, kicks, darkness,
night? Then follow me down
to the place where it hurts,
where politics get dirty
and primitive

in between jazz riffs
where you will hear the question
of how cool should you really get

Negration in Harlem

ex-coloured invisible man
Joe X Caliban
mulatta of a negroid dad
living in exile,
mongoloid void

so how come I heard
in Harlem's no lack?
that the girls vary
with faces of sweet black
berry at night
when veils fall
to let them come to pass

I traveled back
loving night and not knowing
why, tried to
make myself black
thinking it would lead to
excavation of soul
through jazz poem after jazz poem

but all I get is a Toomer
doom, realizing
where the richness and lack like
bride and groom
make up my people

they sing their own old tune
transmuted into the songs once
of rivers, somewhere between

the old rivers and current storms
but I do not follow

their words verging
on madness, am not mad
just tired of dream-talk,
double-speak.

Malcolm X you marked the spot
where I never am

or am I generation exoticized
and x-rated? my people who have been
x-rayed and x-filed
x-chromosomes that missed
the boat, miscegenated awhile
debating destinies not their own?

Catch a Tiger

Jack be nimble,
Jack be quick,
black or white
best take your pick

Boy, your body is a toy
and can't nobody catch you
against the blue black fences
of your lack

You're already beat –
no need to get down with town,
you're already full of stars
like the great Southern night

Its cosmic frailty
the body of your mother
or your lover
sweet as earth

But boy you just don't know
you a man, Jack,
and that I am your daughter,
daddy Mack

I play piano with two hands,
have always
been good at performing,
and when I sleep

I close half my eyes
dream half moons and fingernails
and pretend
I'm meeting you tomorrow morn,

That I'm going to go to the station
without bags
and catch the train
leaving myself behind.

In Other Words

others and not some speak naturally of difference in
syntax/rhythm,
imagery traveling avenues beyond word/poems
that resist and cannot resist open rooms,
spaces that write themselves from the inside like music
    the beauty of incongruence
of off-beat beautiful black women who disappear
in the rain/come back asking you to play it again
    instead of being asked to scatter like rats or
make love in burning tenements or love back
getting kicked down stairs for men's kicks
crossing roads trying to walk like white folk
so they won't get killed but after all these years
    phantasmal veils remain and the mothers of mulatta
children forever
stain the streets writhing 'til dawn. they won't be written
about and that's the only certain thing about them
    but it is precisely their poetry we cannot forget
those local haunts of history,
of woman after woman giving birth to
unholy ghosts of the third species
who keep their laughter sounding like blues.
mothers who got little time for Holiday
even less for Fitzgerald and Piaf and we
could never kill the fathers who stayed
    O Plath why did you become another good bitch
who has to die before she gets put in books
then again why did we die and never get put anywhere.
    we have lived so close to ovens
    getting our skins cooked so the myth goes

but myths are what have killed us, have
replaced our language with arguments for speech
with no right to exist in verse/only controversy
who talk to themselves, whose hearts are somewhere
in Alcatraz hot-blooded but firm,
calling me in my sleep across horizons
singing *shange, shange, shange!* never shantih cuz
I take to rich brown soil and the devil knows I
am not one for paradiso anyway I am still on the
first step trying to break from darkness and
the lightness that has for so long silenced it.
I am trying to break away from circumstance,
trying to break down and further down
and eventually
through

New York, My Future Love

I.

I pray for the dark and your dream each night
hoping to find your streets decked out
in glorious neons and steam, have dreamed
many times of your body singing me into chaos
and peace, have learned to love
the sound of your underground
radiation constant vicious hiss like sacrifice
before marriage, knowing I may resent
only the look of shut eyes in morning when the
text of your body will have given me so many
poems and lives much more than soggy petals
on a black bough. you come and go like Eliot's women,
you smash the precious rock
of ignorance and a great part of me lusts over your
strangers with city faces who blur and desert me forever
each time, but I think the creation of strangers is for you
like making love and I see each street like a lover
I'll have to recover from by evening, will still dream of
in the aftermath of a day's quarrelling, hope to see again
in the event of awake.

II.

The first time I get to you
I sit, able only to take a sip or two
of this coffee as I plunge
my ink to the sound of cabs and Kerouac,
knowing this is the only way
I might just get free. It's a gift
to finally see you,
you who are somewhere between an ex-lover
who hovers in one's consciousness,
and a new affair entirely.
I like that you hardly sleep and throw out
so many poems. I like that you live
at the frontlines of being, your chaotic shrieks
like melody encompassing me by night
and by morning the beauty of waking up
next to you as precious as angels
bringing me up and away to the slapdash beauty of the rain.

Historicizing

look here! what you axing?
what question you still got
I told you I ain't black nor white
your questions keep coming down like knives
but this is my blood, suckers!
it came from eddystone meat packers,
where my grandfather still works nearing eighty,
before that the trans-atlantic sea sickness
leaving Europa
even before that the Pythagorean gore
of the sun setting red across waters
    middle passage is where I was born
maps like skin mean nothing.

Eia, I Am

I.

You came to us like hydrangea
through which a dark world
of secret light began. I remember
the tears that eventually rusted into remembrance
of the heavens where our art
struggled to arrive.

You came to us as tempest, a curse
that did not understand
the meaning
of give in and bend,
even with all those chains
struggled to survive. I grew up

as the eldest daughter, my father echoing
your old song
struggling to make the others conscious
and warm their concavity of spines.
Still the syllables of your name,
mon ami,

have dreamt me into being
and dream. And I have never believed
your poetry to have been obscene
as they assumed. It was just too unafraid,
lashing out like an angry river
or flame;

not that you destroyed,
but that you promised new

seeds, to scare the ignorance out of us
and shed light on the silent
wicked thing race was,
in its blackfaces and white.

You came to us as spasm, spark
in the night,
a murmuring fire that swallowed
my old self, entered my shadow
and then told me to refuse it

letting go of my hand so that I might
thrust its terror into the skies,
awaken and rise across plains of ashes.
I still see you
in every blue welding flame
calling our name.

II.

now that you're gone there is something
about the words culture and blackness

that escapes me that I can no longer identify.
the idea of dismantling the myth seems necessary

so as to break free, but I have been taught
that identity means oppression. now

that you're gone there is a whole dark world
to learn, an emptiness about nature that makes

my return to roots illogical. somehow the negress
in me repressed by the ease with which

I have been white all these years. I may have
the attitude necessary for your movement,

have embodied the shadow of your Martinique
and for many years struggled with the destiny

I hope will continue to progressively cadaver
itself, like the jewel of la France

which your ghost continues to overthrow.
at the end of daybreak I never imagined

your own expiration in a pool of silence
but that's life. at the end of daybreak

the overture carries me through and suddenly
the song continues, and not an inch of this world

is devoid of your fingerprint, *the vitelline*
membrane of my future children

giving way to the great waters
I hope will rebirth us all.

III.

O, you were always that tumultuous trio
of eyes:

the man who broke through ontology
but had the strong bones and soul
to match, who came through the storm
as fire bringing water.
It was you
and I knew this because the world
was suddenly ready to empty itself
of silence, was altogether too full
of empty gourds and fools,
arms stretched out sleeping

and too much kneeling, needing fewer
domesticated souls.

Now getting home
to a house without you I pull
the curtains back to the clamor
of the day, staring at the grey

and your death,
neither tower nor cathedral
but something that takes root
in the red flesh of the earth,
aftermath of the sun –

I pull the curtains back

the world a stage now
estranged from itself, and from the light
which is now fading
to black,

my skin unbroken
but also unexplored. I sing

Eia

for you who never conquered
anything but captivated all

Eia

for all the songs you brought for us
to soften the weary fall

but Eia does not lessen my weariness –
is a gesture of madness
for the world left behind
deep with disbelief and defeats
doubling as victories.

I hope that at least
what you carried with you
was neither laughter nor screams
but the single note of prophecy:

Eia

a note that plays forever
and does not flinch, sings forever
until the ship and shore cinch
into a metaphysical breaking

apart, and then a breakthrough
of the heart:

horizons still red
with the geometry of old wounds

but still singing
we must accept

if we expect to live. Still living
you tell me to accept

and I will, watch me
as I sing your song
into the storm.

Rosetti's Girl at a Latrice, 1862

My mouth repeating itself
into scream, into the eventual
constellations that vacationers would grow
to wish on,
we stared angrily from gutters

Wondering how many prophets were killed
in the great silhouette of your strength,
how many of my mulatrices
died in the latrices
of your gloria mundi

Your sweet face like Beatrice
transposed into an arrangement of points
a psychology orange and sad,
ornamenting itself in nights

When my great great grandfathers
prepared their own soil;
what structure of you can hold
Huis Clos?
your gaze, behind iron lacing
imagining hell as other people
never right here

Canary in the Mine

there is a certain uncertainty
to things
nobody knows

except me that
I either turn white
out of pride or fright

or disappear: that's right,
I am the canary
in the coal mine

I tell you how poisonous race politics
get, and if it gets
too bad I die

I warn you: we're all going down!
this is no song, no harmony is found here,
my death will have been the manifestation

of your symptoms, your nation!
we who survive
will be least alive

Béatrix

I.

girl you should have never walked those streets
till dawn with that skin,
shoulda kept singin' –

not the gospel, apocalypse,
but some mulatta song,

dialectic of light and dark and
hopefully light again

like how you must have felt
coming back from Palazzo Cenci
washed up like that

your body barely showing
against the pale harvest
but your ghost sharp,
abandoning itself

to Rome
where you did what Romans wouldn't do,
the kind of person your father was,
the romance of origins
that never caught you

sometimes I catch myself
wishing I could have saved you
or myself

but now no one shall think
of your September death

amidst the fields
churning into gulfs,

soon to become journal entries, cursive
words like scars

no one will hear your voice
bringing news of ancestors
who bled through graves

exiles in their own soil,
and the rest of us waiting
for revolution

let them carry their heads in a basket
while you and I traverse the dawn,

walk in on those old haunts
in haggard heels, hoping to be
the children of the gods
and not of the odds

let us go to those waters
still alive and black
those rivers
where you can always see the city
where we can entertain thoughts
of lovers we never had nor will.

II.

blessed one,
you were either my
literary double
or another kind of lover
twixt night and day,
Renaissance and Generation X
your music gone
but underground we carry on

For Gerard

You must have been my soul mate,
not because you were a dead French poet
or that we both had stuffy last names,
but that you were ashamed
God could see you.
You were never ashamed of your pet
lobster, though, which people said you brought on walks,
or that you spent your life looking
for the Queen of Sheba in your dreams
on any given afternoon. I, too, have longed for her,
calling it my journey into self,
have longed for those who know the secrets
of the sea, have believed in light
and not God
as the precursor to socialism.
If we had met in Paris on some
black and white night,
I know things would have fallen into life.

Old Comrade, Lover

It was a common night I decided love
should never again
begin with these gestures:
a soft touch, whispers, eyelashes,
to proceed in laughable style.

Instead I figured we could dance
over the hollows
where we were born, and to the cry
of pride over prejudice,
over barricades high enough
for us to escape the decadence
and sleep
like two visions of Picasso,
curvatures sharp

dancing through the mines
in a kind of love
that cannot be mapped into place or poem
but will lift its head
from flesh, will remark on bourgeois decadence
sing heavily and grow
sober with the night.

A kind of love that
is not flipping through photographs
or willing ourselves
into practicality. It will be
a love as graceful as ghosts of
El Shabbaz,
ready for the apocalypse

for it is with eyes unveiled
that I have learned this music
of deepest understanding,
the distance which has
only placed our exchanges deliberately
at the frontline of the spirit.

Petit Jean

It was a rainy day in Lowell
when I saw you waiting in the cab.
I ran towards you, fierce rain drops soaking into fine leather,
    Edison Cemetery, I wheezed.
You asked the same old question,
    So who you visiting? Friend, family, or what?
    A little of each, I replied.
You laughed lazily and I kept

to myself, thinking how my poor Ti Jean
died so misunderstood, and so young.
Clutching a secret quart
of champagne we found the grave,
and I walked out into the rain.
You stayed

with your engine on, somehow understanding.
Nobody wants to visit cemeteries
when the weather's bad.
I remember how you got out, coatless,
to help me find the stone.
    It's probably covered in cigarettes and leaves,
you said, I remember your white sneakers also,
turning brown and your face
red with a strange determination.
I remember how you couldn't tell I was shaking.

    Then there it was,

there I was
out of breath trying to find his body,
as if I had been running all over America,

I said goodbye to you and hello to Jack,
waiting for you to drive off and leave me
there in a strange peace
but you never did.

I remember staying a good twenty minutes to
speak to the keeper of my dreams
and that you stayed, saying nothing,
understanding everything such as the irony
of how quiet the earth was then: no laugh, no hullabaloo
of his legacy in sight,
just the cold grey drone of the day
the rain weighing down on our bones.
    "He honored life" it read

and it was there I understood love,
the golden eternity (X marks the spot).

When I walked back to your cab
you told me not to worry about it.
With a slight buzz I watched your taxi lights guide me back
like two saints, and suddenly your confession:
    Yeah, I knew Kerouac when I was your age, we used to go for beers just up that road.

I laughed to keep from crying

and you laughed that lazy laugh, mentioning
that he was much quieter
than we would think , a shrinking violet
until the wine.
    But he loved himself!
and these words I will remember.

At the train station I shook your hand,
my heart burning at 5 p.m.
and I asked you what your name was.
You smiled.

Jack. Funny, ain't it! Tell them folks up in Toronto about me.

And then everything in place like God.

Holler

I've seen the best minds of my generation
twice removed
twice destroyed by cranial measurements
fixed on negroes
living on streets beside old brownstones,
my imaginary daughters dancing to hollow ex-coloured man-
made
rhythms with pale blue eyes
masking black skins making up
for lost authenticities approximated
in jazz lingo many males like Mailer didn't understand;
who passed through classifications not understanding
lexicons of madness getting a Master's in English
in Massachusetts university classrooms
to become massas, to just get in
and pass, and survive
as the subjects of sidelong looks and
white caesuras like the history books
ending in questions infinite;
who closed their eyes and chests like oysters
hiding pearls and broken bones,
other strange fruits and moons;
who were born like poems,
dust in corners, created in hearsay
in the details of the great Myth, visible in the face of the gods;
who whispered *now let us put the fragments*
into another self
the sound of the sea between the CBC
tightening into the fist of America;
we who have longed for an American self only now
that we can build a kingdom out of our old tragic
selves; we who have been waiting
to become the fire of general universes,
to dance on the edge of matter
with bodies colliding like old stars ready to
die; we who have spent lives trying to
catch up with uncountable time,
waiting for the right sentence to attach

while we bound ourselves like books
strewn down alleys reading from Brooklyn
to 125th's hydrogen red like you've never seen;
we who never saw with eyes except veiled whiskey
eyes that drained the pain but also our brilliance
fading into the artificial bright of night;
we who have altered moons and
attested to the lunar era of your mind,
the pesky voice of conscience of scientific mishap
craniometry dreams screaming apologies but
we are not listening; we who have been whipped
into bent syllables
like lightning, like breathing streets
of a red tamarind dawn;
we who bleed against the maroon skies which
we eventually become, the skies of our fathers,
and live
with the rinds of love,
against the television buzz, against the
silence your heart ain't never heard,
and down, down like the surrender of rain;
we who have traveled dry-mouthed in the backs of cabs
stomachs burning at 3 a.m.
like scavengers of love, looking for love, *hello, love*
but really just watching tired couples lingering
in the lasso of the sun, hoping to find
ourselves;
we who implode like chinaberry trees,
uncaged songs of compassion,
cubist confessions on bended knee
our lives one long Blue Period;
we who have tried to believe in Josephine
when she said we are all just two arms, two legs, a stomach and
a head
but we have lost the arms, the guts and the head
in order to see through the Veil, hauntings,
problems of love and understanding

that have prevented us from vibrating into cosmic harmonies;
we who are looking for roots
already pulled, for a way out of
destinies already doomed;
we who fill rooms with our absence,
are invisible with colour, who have learned to live
with poets because they are the only ones who see
how heaven emerges
in the debris, in the earth when it lays itself
open and naked
in the unpretentiously early morn,
poets who are the only ones who see us;
we who mourn when the wine is gone, who laugh
to keep from the realization that we were always
meant to be alone;
we who are sea grass, shadow dance,
the general rhythm of things,
the abandoned children born
who have not yet admitted light;
we who have lived and died by confession
while waiting to hear God's,
the Great Poem a mere negotiation of what leaves
and what must stay, the miracle of death
a choice and our life a negotiation
of our death;
we who are drunk and starving for friends
who will not forget us
as we forget ourselves against skylines
waiting for a moment where we may outlive;
we who are the black holes of bloodroots,
codes and sea-songs across voyages
of exile; we who have only known exile
and are triumphing
triumphing against it
as tree, rock, soil,
map, womb, hieroglyph,
Amen.

Anno Domini

Your tragedy was ours, the one of generations
    of men and women who could no longer be prepared
for the world, the tragedy of a world

that becomes apparent to us because it repeats itself. I think
    of you when others sleep,
crawling into the crevices of Trinity

College where you often hid, imagining a time, your time,
    when the human world penetrated into the heavenly,
a place where air was music

and grief was something we wrote down.
    In your absence I understand why there is a time and place
for scepticism, why every blank page is a prayer

awaiting our hands.
    Why nothing is ever the same old, and why you worked late
into the night as a prayer for the rest of us

who sleepwalk because it is always more dangerous to live.
    But I do not fully understand
why you do not live, will most likely live only by asking

this question. If it is true, as you said, that doubt means
    freedom then I will pray not for the answer but for the
strength to invoke your name,

in a resolve to keep burning, take hold of the awareness
    you said was inside all of us, preceded Creation.
In the flesh of my palm your universe

which never left me, the paradise which has always been
    here. After you left I heard you say
we may want only for the angels to watch over us

but what if they are merely wrestling for our attention
    in orbs
of everyday light.

for A.D., in memoriam

Prism Woman

every turn seems a wearing away, smoothing my sides
    down
washed up on the shore always hesitating, burning. this river a
sight, the streets still yonder, still the rotting ship,
glimpses of the barefoot earth masked in ancient
armour, still the water unquenched with blood, prisons
of the body. I am a woman of many sides and sidelong looks,
my angles are alternating
in shape and sharpness provoking the edges
where most of us choose to reel back. I cut myself
and others out and in without siding with anybody,
my sides always chasing the curve
of a dream. besides, which side of a river is right
and which left if it runs through a sterile earth,
an earth still stumbling on old blood myths
waiting for us to choose against the Veil
and try walking on those waters whose asides
are barbarous laughter. it is all a lacy mixture
of two sides and no side, an outside
    I learn to live in.
it is an exilic paradise I can pass through,
bleeding across the invisible and coloured lines
those strange divides and feral fields where I was born
and reside and resist.

Blanqueamiento

The land that's yours is mine,
is shadows, which I see
both dreaming and in the night
when drums make our old selves dance,
bring us to embrace those old ghosts
weaving through. No one owns them
or us,
    nor the fearful asymmetries
of our lineage, of our Caribe we left
for new callings,
    a new response
from Yoruba to Cuba we work hard
to reflect. This land that's yours
is a patria of poes'a mulata;
    we shan't forget
these shanty towns, this Afroantillana
beyond the pale, beyond even Matos
and Guillén there is a spirit
unlearning its colour and shade, becoming
the mantilla we pull out
from the eyes,
challenging the dark.

What else to say in this assortment of
motion, stars,
this strange green sky,
waiting for the train

in the certainty of night:
these may be the last grey days
where light bends

through glass and the spring
and is reborn again,
wandering

among names of the dead, remembering
the peace of communion,
the landscapes which fade

at the edges but hold our bodies in place,
the letters written in a furtive ink
stitching promises
    of pilgrimage,

towards the sea that calls
me to embark
into a dialectic of light and dark,

and then hopefully light again,
back to the theories and poems we wept for

a true pledge for morning,
for the momentum to run,
to sing as a way of traveling

to await only
the moment where all that is static
shatters into hope.

Exegesis

my grandmother promised me
diamonds
in exchange for communion
I wondered if those diamonds
would be as forever
as the guilt
that has sewn itself into her bones

my father
too socialist for the spirit, too realist for Hegel
but whose religion you could call
the beginning, father of fathers
who brought me
Axum and witchcraft movies
supporting either lifestyle choice

my mother
whose body is shaped like a world
and who came from so many other
strega nonnas, before the burnings
or the script,
when there was still enough faith left
to heal by heart and hands alone

my uncle who believed in God
da Vinci
C* algebras
and the stars, constellations
the only pattern
that could understand
his mind

my sister
who kids and threatens me with a mad look
that she'll join a nunnery
if I don't close her
door goodnight
and whose looks rival Makeda
in even her sweeter reincarnations

as for myself
I am somewhere between
Abyssinia and Israel,
between the Sun God and the trickster
whose jokes are so long
we become afraid to laugh,
I try to laugh sometimes
when I can't pray, try to sing
the prayer into things
try to dance rather than chant
or wait to levitate like the movies
and if that doesn't work
find a new light to resolve.

Exigere

they may try to shape us into negative space,
to separate us from consciousness but also the
extimatrix called home, that good old exile
for which there is no science, no axiom,
for which there is no inside/outside
only an interior excess
called soul
which must become the mold
of movement, of moving from dark catastrophe
or the pale face of frailty
to the dynamic moment
where we let newness enter the world,
and they see how we have parted seas
daily for centuries.

Ex-

the prefix ex-
like pre-ordained fixing of my
mixedness,
seemingly signifying something
increasingly
old
or gone

like throw my people towards the exit (back door)
calling their right to exist
a question of either/or,
like exaggerated exclaims
about the best of two worlds
signifying how this world
was not made for us

ex- like deus ex machina
like eccentric, ex-centric
ex-patriate mamacita,
like I have to keep explaining myself
    but how do I explain
using lexicons of *l'anglais*?
ex- like creation out of nothing

like the miscegenation taboo,
like Othello, the first existentialist,
ex- like the excess
margin of Canada's exonerating
anti-racist memoir, like the exclusion and execution
of my Mohawk spirit,

ex- like the old news
of newcomers desiring
to exorcise their blackness, like white negro hip
but at what expense?
no experimentation with passing
can pass

ex- like
we either expire or explode
into history and get remembered
instead of tip-toe
towards the necessary
exeunt.

Notes

P. 51 Gerard Nerval's last words, "Do not wait up for me this evening, for the night will be black and white." Richard Sieburth, *Gerard de Nerval: Selected Writings.* London: Penguin Group, 1999. p. xxxi.

P. 57 "Holler" is inspired by Allen Ginsberg's *Howl.*

"Now the fragments have been put together again by another self." Frantz Fanon, *Black Skins, White Masks.* New York: Grove Press, 1967. p.109.

ADEBE D.A. is a writer whose words travel between Toronto and New York City. She recently completed her MA at York University, where she also served as Assistant Editor for the arts and literary journal, *Existere*. Her work has been published in various North American sources, such as *Canadian Woman Studies Journal*, *The Claremont Review*, *Canadian Literature, CV2* and *The Toronto Star*. She won the Toronto Poetry Competition in 2005 to become Toronto's first Junior Poet Laureate. *Ex Nihilo* is her debut collection.